NNAT®
GRADE 2
(NNAT3 Level C)

ABOUT ORIGINS PUBLICATIONS

Origins Publications helps students develop their higher-order thinking skills while also improving their chances of admission into gifted and accelerated learner programs.

Our goal is to unleash and nurture the genius in every student. We do this by offering educational and test prep materials that are fun, challenging and provide a sense of accomplishment.

Please contact us with any questions.
info@originspublications.com

Copyright© 2019 by Origins Publications
Written and Edited by: Gifted and Talented NNAT Test Prep Team

All rights reserved. This book or any portion thereof may not be reproduced or used in any manner whatsoever without the express written permission of the publisher.

ISBN: 978-1-948255-82-0

The Naglieri Nonverbal Ability Test® (NNAT®) is a registered trademark of NCS Pearson Inc., which is not affiliated with Origins Publications. NCS Pearson Inc. has not endorsed the contents of this book.

BONUS

DOWNLOAD YOUR NNAT PRACTICE TEST

IN

COLOR

If you also want the COLOR version of this book, please go to the following link to download it!

Please visit

https://originstutoring.lpages.co/nnat130

to access the color version of the practice test.

Contents

Part 1. Introduction to the NNAT® 4

    Who Takes The NNAT® Level C? 4

    When Does the NNAT® Take Place? 4

    NNAT® Level C Overview 4

        Length 4

        Format 4

Part 2. How To Use This Book 4

Part 3: Test Prep Tips and Strategies 5

Part 4: Question Types and Teaching Tips 6

NNAT® Level C Practice Test One 13

Bubble Sheets & Answer Keys 31

Part 1: Introduction to the NNAT®

This book offers an overview of the types of questions on the Naglieri Nonverbal Ability Test (NNAT) Level C, test-taking strategies to improve performance, and one full-length practice NNAT® Level C practice test that students can use to assess their knowledge and practice their test-taking skills.

Who Takes the NNAT® Level C?

The NNAT® Level C is often used as an assessment tool or admissions test in 2nd grade for entry into 3rd grade of gifted and talented programs and highly-competitive schools. The NNAT® Level C is also used as an assessment tool by teachers to figure out which students would benefit from an accelerated or remedial curriculum.

When Does the NNAT® Take Place?

This depends on the school district you reside in or want to attend. Check with the relevant school/district to learn more about test dates and the application/ registration process.

NNAT® Level C Overview

The NNAT® is designed to assess the cognitive skills that relate to academic success in school for students between four and 18. The questions on the NNAT® consist of geometric figures, shapes, and symbols. A child must use visual reasoning and logical thinking to decipher the answers. The test does not require a child to be able to read, write or speak in the English Language.

Length

The NNAT® has 48 multiple-choice questions and offers both an online version and a paper and pencil test. It takes approximately 30 minutes to complete.

Format

The official NNAT® test has only 3 colors: blue, orange and green. (The color green was recently added in the most recent edition of the NNAT). This book is in black and white, but you can download the color version from our website. Get the link from the page at the begining or end of this book.

Part 2: How to Use this Book

The NNAT® is an important test and the more a student is familiar with the questions on the exam, the better she will fare when taking the test.

This book will help your student get used to the format and content of the test so s/he will be adequately prepared and feel confident on test day.

Inside this book, you will find:

- Overview of each question type on the test and teaching tips to help your child approach each question type strategically and with confidence.

- 1 full-length NNAT® Level C practice test and answer keys.

Part 3. Test Prep Tips and Strategies

Firstly, and most importantly, commit to make the test preparation process a stress-free one. A student's ability to keep calm and focused in the face of challenge is a quality that will benefit him or her throughout his or her academic life.

Be prepared for difficult questions from the get-go! There will be a certain percentage of questions that are very challenging for all children. It is key to encourage students to use all strategies available when faced with challenging questions. And remember that a student can get quite a few questions wrong and still do very well on the test.

Before starting the practice test, go through the sample questions and read the general test prep strategies provided at the beginning of the book. They will help you guide your student as he or she progresses through the practice test.

The following strategies may also be useful as you help your child prepare:

Before You Start

- Find a quiet, comfortable spot to work free of distractions.
- Tell your student you will be doing some fun activities.
- Show your student how to perform the simple technique of shading (and erasing) bubbles.

During Prep

- Encourage your student to carefully consider all the answer options before selecting one. Tell him or her there is only ONE answer.
- Encourage your student to visualise the correct answer in the empty box before checking the answer options.
- If your student is stumped by a question, she or he can use the process of elimination. First, encourage your student to eliminate obviously wrong answers to narrow down the answer choices. If your student is still in doubt after using this technique, tell him or her to guess as there are no points deducted for wrong answers.

- If challenged by a question, ask your student to explain why he or she chose a specific answer. If the answer was incorrect, this will help you identify where your student is stumbling. If the answer was correct, asking your student to articulate her reasoning aloud will help reinforce the concept.
- Review all the questions your student answered incorrectly, and explain to your student why the answer is incorrect. Have your student attempt these questions again a few days later to see if he or she now understands the concept.
- Encourage your student to do his or her best, but take plenty of study breaks. Start with 10-15 minute sessions. Your student will perform best if she views these activities as fun and engaging, not as exercises to be avoided.

When to Start Preparing?

Every family and student will approach preparation for this test differently. There is no 'right' way to prepare; there is only the best way for a particular child and family. We suggest students take one full-length practice test and spend 6-8 hours reviewing NNAT® practice questions.

If you have limited time to prepare, spend most energy reviewing areas where your student is encountering the majority of problems.

As they say, knowledge is power! Preparing for the NNAT® will certainly help your student avoid anxiety and make sure she does not give up too soon when faced with unfamiliar and perplexing questions.

Part 4: Question Types and Teaching Tips

The NNAT® Level C is comprised of four different question types:

Pattern Completion
Reasoning by Analogy
Serial Reasoning
Spatial Visualization

Each question type involves the following steps:

- The student is presented with a picture of a matrix.
- The student must observe and detect the relationship among the parts of the matrix.
- The student must solve the problem based on the information shown to her within the matrix, and choose the correct answer from five possible options.

Pattern Completion

With this question type, the student is presented with a design in a rectangle. Inside the large

Introduction to the NNAT®

rectangle is a smaller white rectangle representing a missing piece that completes the design. The student must choose the answer that best fits the inner rectangle so that the missing parts complete the design.

These questions are the most common question types found on the Level A and B tests, and they are the easiest kinds of matrices in the exam. On the Level C exam, these question types appear relatively less frequently.

When your students encounters this kind of question for the first few times, say:

"Look at the picture. A piece is missing where you see the question mark. Show me the piece that is missing in the answer choices."

After seeing these questions a few times, your student will probably not need this prompt and will spontaneously point to or mark an answer.

SAMPLE QUESTION:

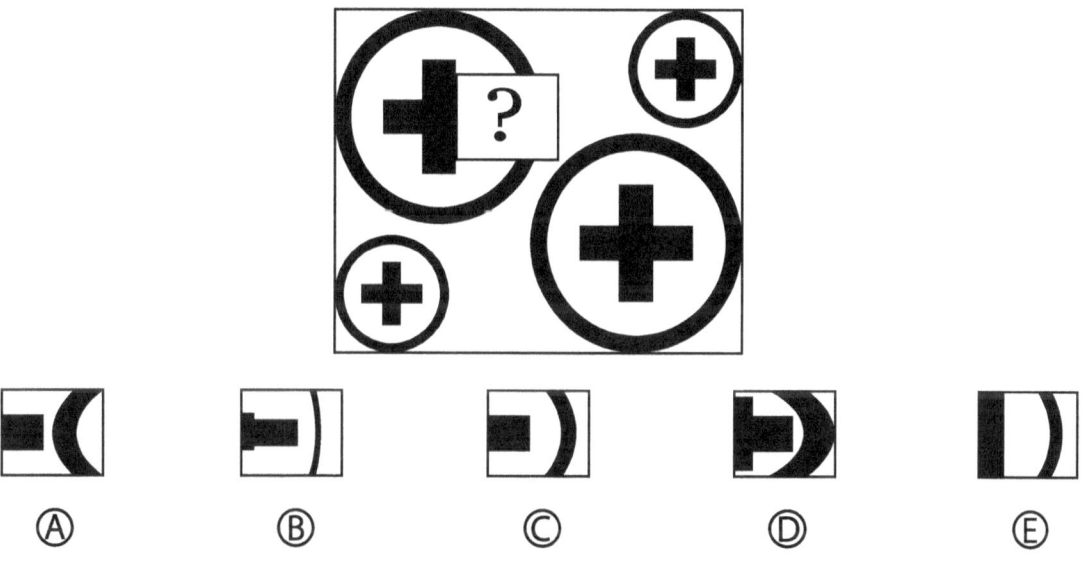

Answer: C

TIPS:

Ask your student to complete the picture by continuing the correct lines and colors of the design into the empty box. Then, match the drawing with the correct answer choice.

Ask your student to note the color/shade and design next to the corners of the empty box as this is a useful base to help identify the correct answer.

Go through each answer option and ask the student to visualize how each choice would fit the design.

Reasoning by Analogy

With this question type, the child is presented with a matrix of 4-6 boxes containing objects, usually geometric shapes.

To solve the problem, the child must determine how the object changes as it moves across the row and down the column in the matrix. The question may require that the student pay close attention to several aspects of the design (e.g: shading, color, shape) at the same time.

When your students encounters this kind of question for the first few times, say:

"Look at the picture. A piece is missing where you see the question mark. Show me the piece that is missing in the answer choices."

SAMPLE QUESTION:

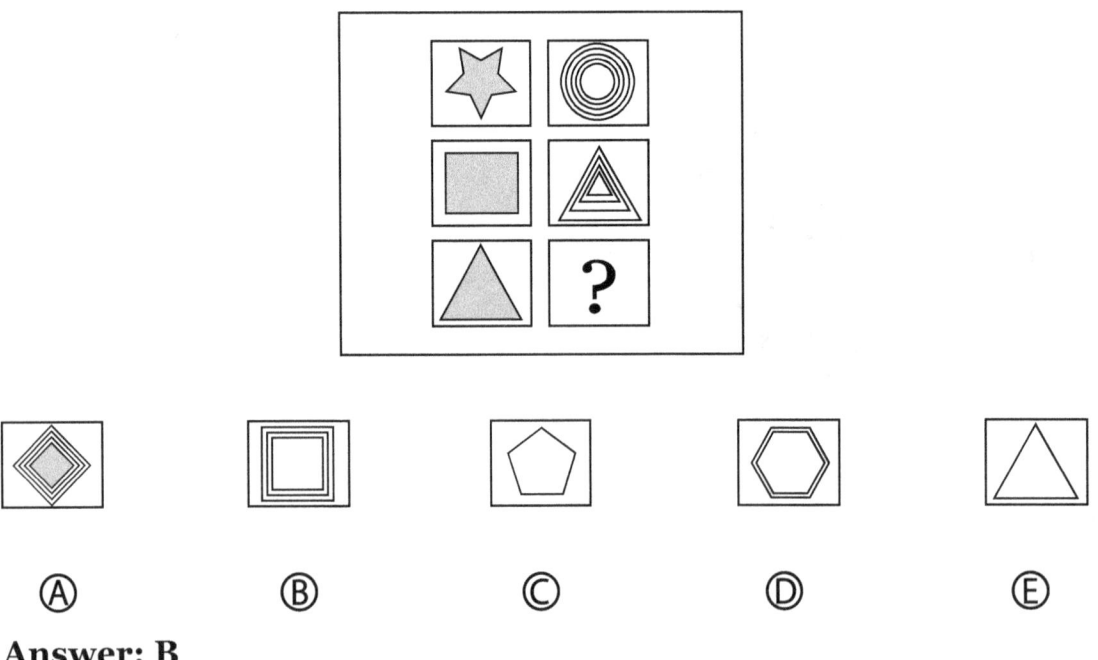

Answer: B

TIPS:
Make sure your student knows key concepts that come up in these types of questions, including geometric concepts such as rotational symmetry, line symmetry, parts of a whole.

If your student is finding these items difficult, encourage her to discover the pattern by looking in each direction (horizontally and vertically).
- Ask: "How do the objects change in the first row? Do you see a pattern? Do the objects change in the same way in the second row? The third row?"
- Ask: "How do the objects change in the first column? Do you see a pattern? Do the objects change in the same way in the second column? The third column?"

Introduction to the NNAT®

Encourage your student to isolate one element (e.g: outer shape, inner shape/s) and identify how it changes:
- Is the color/shading of the element changing as it moves?
- Is the element changing positions as it moves? Does it move up or down? Clockwise or counter-clockwise? Does it end up in the opposite (mirror) position?
- Does the element disappear and appear again as it move along the row/ column? Does it get bigger or smaller?

Encourage your student to make a prediction for the missing object and compare the description with the answer choices.

Serial Reasoning

With this question type, the student is shown a series of shapes that change across the rows and columns throughout the design. These questions require the student to understand how the objects in rows and columns relate to each other. The student must isolate and apply the rule/s in order to identify which object from the answer choices fits the empty box in the bottom right-hand corner of the matrix.

When your students encounters this kind of question for the first few times, say:

"Look at the picture. A piece is missing where you see the question mark. Show me the piece that is missing in the answer choices."

SAMPLE QUESTION:

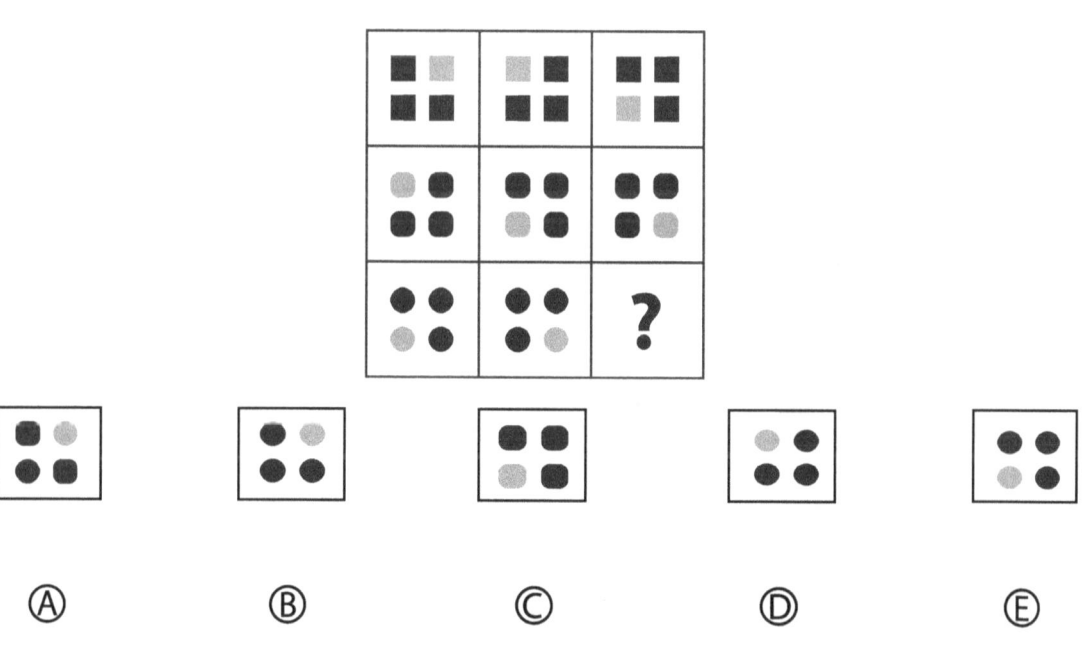

Answer: B

Introduction to the NNAT®

TIPS:
Encourage your student to discover the pattern by looking in each direction.
• Ask: "How do the objects change in the first row (or first column)? Do you see a pattern? Do the objects change in the same way in the second row (or second column)? The third row (or third column)?"
• Diagonally (if the item is a 6-box matrix). Ask: "How do the objects change across the diagonal? Do you see a pattern?"

Encourage your student to isolate one element and identify how it changes.
• How does the color/shading of the element change as it moves along the row/column?
• Does the element change positions as it moves along the row/column? Does it move up, down or around (i.e.: clockwise, counter-clockwise). Does the element move to the opposite position?
• Does the element get bigger, smaller or stay the same as it moves? Does the element disappear and appear again as you move along the row/column?

Spatial Visualization

With this question type, a student is presented with a series of objects that combine, invert, transform and/or rotate across rows and columns. The student must identify the rule for the top row of objects and then predict what will happen to objects in the second (or third) row. Spatial Visualization items are widely seen to be the most difficult, particularly when involving objects that intersect in ways that are hard to recognize or involve an object rotating.

When your students encounters this kind of question for the first few times, say:

"A piece is missing where you see the question mark. Show me the missing piece in the answer choices."

SAMPLE QUESTION:

    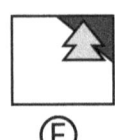
　　Ⓐ　　　　　　Ⓑ　　　　　　Ⓒ　　　　　　Ⓓ　　　　　　Ⓔ

Answer: A

TIPS:

Ask your student to do some paper-folding projects. This will help her understand how objects on a folded piece of paper appear (and relate to each other) when the paper is opened.

Encourage your student to visualize -- observe, imagine and keep track of -- the changes in the geometric shapes as they move and then draw what she predicts she might see in the empty box.

Encourage your student to isolate one element (e.g: outer shape, inner shape/s) and identify how it changes.
- How does the color/shading of the element change as it moves along the row/column?
- Does the element change positions as it moves along the row/column?Does the element move to the opposite position?
- Does the element flip positions (e.g.: outer square becomes inner square or vice-versa)? Does the element go upside down?
- Does the element combine with another element?

NNAT® C Practice Test One

Answer bubble sheets can be found at the back of the book. Please make sure your student fills in each of the bubbles fully.

10

11

12

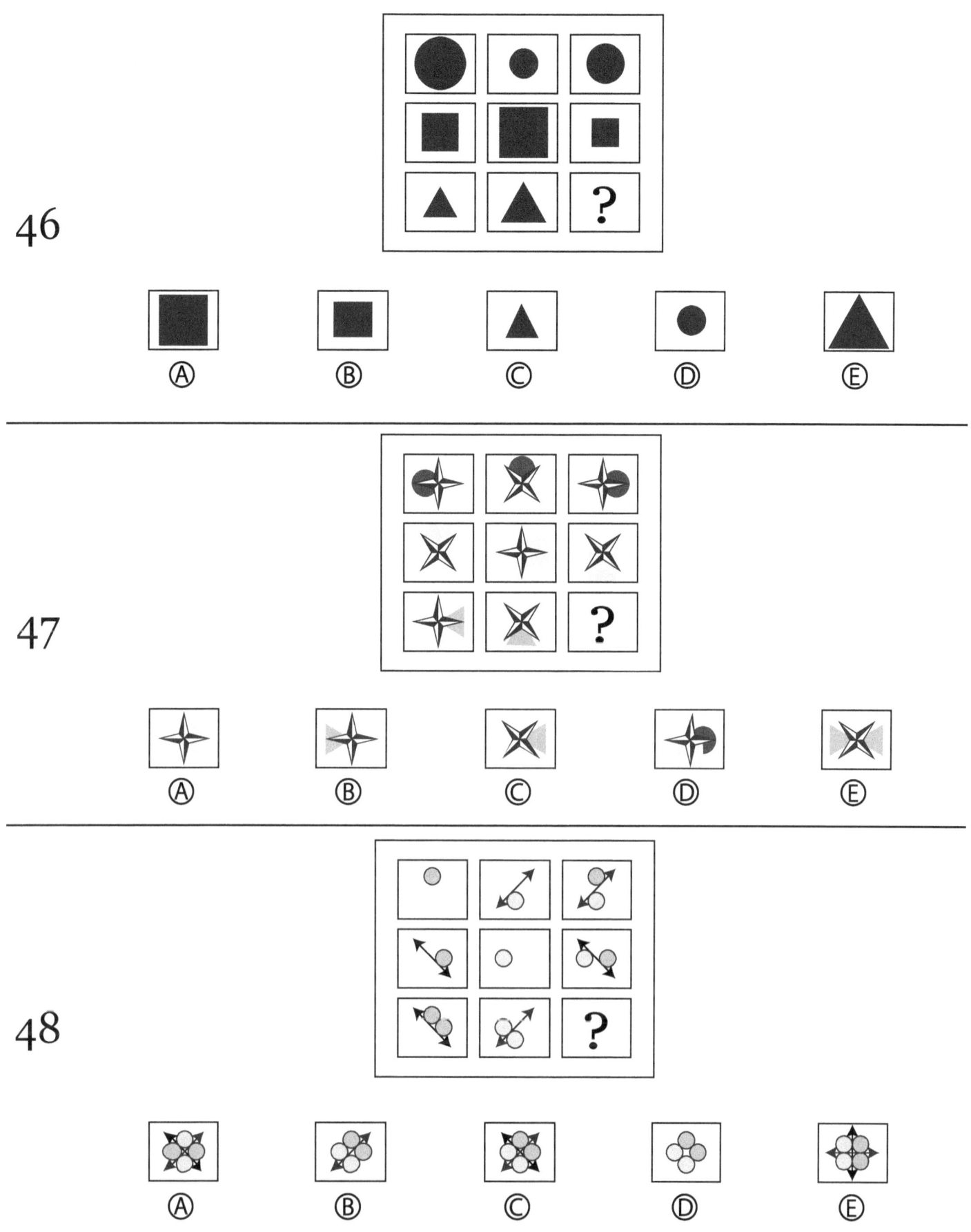

NNAT® Level C Bubble Sheet & Answer Explanations

Practice Test One

Use a No. 2 Pencil
Fill in bubble completely.
Ⓐ ● Ⓒ Ⓓ

Name:_____ Date:_____

1. Ⓐ Ⓑ Ⓒ Ⓓ Ⓔ
2. Ⓐ Ⓑ Ⓒ Ⓓ Ⓔ
3. Ⓐ Ⓑ Ⓒ Ⓓ Ⓔ
4. Ⓐ Ⓑ Ⓒ Ⓓ Ⓔ
5. Ⓐ Ⓑ Ⓒ Ⓓ Ⓔ
6. Ⓐ Ⓑ Ⓒ Ⓓ Ⓔ
7. Ⓐ Ⓑ Ⓒ Ⓓ Ⓔ
8. Ⓐ Ⓑ Ⓒ Ⓓ Ⓔ
9. Ⓐ Ⓑ Ⓒ Ⓓ Ⓔ
10. Ⓐ Ⓑ Ⓒ Ⓓ Ⓔ
11. Ⓐ Ⓑ Ⓒ Ⓓ Ⓔ
12. Ⓐ Ⓑ Ⓒ Ⓓ Ⓔ
13. Ⓐ Ⓑ Ⓒ Ⓓ Ⓔ
14. Ⓐ Ⓑ Ⓒ Ⓓ Ⓔ
15. Ⓐ Ⓑ Ⓒ Ⓓ Ⓔ
16. Ⓐ Ⓑ Ⓒ Ⓓ Ⓔ
17. Ⓐ Ⓑ Ⓒ Ⓓ Ⓔ
18. Ⓐ Ⓑ Ⓒ Ⓓ Ⓔ
19. Ⓐ Ⓑ Ⓒ Ⓓ Ⓔ
20. Ⓐ Ⓑ Ⓒ Ⓓ Ⓔ
21. Ⓐ Ⓑ Ⓒ Ⓓ Ⓔ
22. Ⓐ Ⓑ Ⓒ Ⓓ Ⓔ
23. Ⓐ Ⓑ Ⓒ Ⓓ Ⓔ
24. Ⓐ Ⓑ Ⓒ Ⓓ Ⓔ
25. Ⓐ Ⓑ Ⓒ Ⓓ Ⓔ

26. Ⓐ Ⓑ Ⓒ Ⓓ Ⓔ
27. Ⓐ Ⓑ Ⓒ Ⓓ Ⓔ
28. Ⓐ Ⓑ Ⓒ Ⓓ Ⓔ
29. Ⓐ Ⓑ Ⓒ Ⓓ Ⓔ
30. Ⓐ Ⓑ Ⓒ Ⓓ Ⓔ
31. Ⓐ Ⓑ Ⓒ Ⓓ Ⓔ
32. Ⓐ Ⓑ Ⓒ Ⓓ Ⓔ
33. Ⓐ Ⓑ Ⓒ Ⓓ Ⓔ
34. Ⓐ Ⓑ Ⓒ Ⓓ Ⓔ
35. Ⓐ Ⓑ Ⓒ Ⓓ Ⓔ
36. Ⓐ Ⓑ Ⓒ Ⓓ Ⓔ
37. Ⓐ Ⓑ Ⓒ Ⓓ Ⓔ
38. Ⓐ Ⓑ Ⓒ Ⓓ Ⓔ
39. Ⓐ Ⓑ Ⓒ Ⓓ Ⓔ
40. Ⓐ Ⓑ Ⓒ Ⓓ Ⓔ
41. Ⓐ Ⓑ Ⓒ Ⓓ Ⓔ
42. Ⓐ Ⓑ Ⓒ Ⓓ Ⓔ
43. Ⓐ Ⓑ Ⓒ Ⓓ Ⓔ
44. Ⓐ Ⓑ Ⓒ Ⓓ Ⓔ
45. Ⓐ Ⓑ Ⓒ Ⓓ Ⓔ
46. Ⓐ Ⓑ Ⓒ Ⓓ Ⓔ
47. Ⓐ Ⓑ Ⓒ Ⓓ Ⓔ
48. Ⓐ Ⓑ Ⓒ Ⓓ Ⓔ

NNAT C Test One Answer Explanations.

Please note that there are often various ways to solve the puzzles. These answer explantions provide one option for solving each puzzle.

The answer explanations provide the correct answer for both the 'color' and 'black and white' versions of the book (the black/white/gray shade are referenced, when relevant, in brackets).

Download a color version of this book at:
https://originstutoring.lpages.co/nnat130

1. **D.** The puzzle piece completes the pattern.

2. **D.** The puzzle piece completes the pattern.

3. **B.** The puzzle piece completes the pattern.

4. **B.** Moving across the row, the shape flips across the vertical axis and elongates. The color of the shape and the background color remains the same.

5. **E.** Moving across the row, the shape turns 90 degrees counterclockwise. The color of the shape and the background color remains the same.

6. **E.** The shape alternates between triangle, circle and square across the rows and down the columns. The background color and each shape's color (white) stays the same.

7. **D.** The shape (star) turns 180 degrees from box to box across the rows. Down the columns, the star orientation stays the same as the star's color alternates. The color of the star remains the same across each row.

8. **D.** Each row contains a white box, a shaded/color box, and a box that is half white. The bottom row has a white box and a shaded/color box. Therefore, the bottom right box must have the box that is half white.

9. **D.** Moving across the row from right to left, the reflection of the shape is added across the horizontal axis. (The black line dividing the reflected shapes disappears).

10. **D.** The puzzle piece completes the pattern.

11. **C.** The puzzle piece completes the pattern.

12. **A.** The puzzle piece completes the pattern.

13. **A.** The figures reflect on the 45 degree clockwise axis.

14. **B.** The black figure changes to white, the white figure changes to medium gray (or green), while the backgrounds change from white to medium gray (or green).

15. **C.** The colors of the background and the foreground shapes exchange from left to right.

16. **B.** The shapes combine down each column to form the bottom element while the shapes alternate across the columns.

17. **C.** The shapes alternate across the rows. Down each column, the shapes combine in the first two boxes to complete the shape in the third box. The background colors alternate throughout the matrix.

18. **A.** The shapes combine from bottom to top and from left to right to form the final scene in the top right corner.

19. **E.** The figures outside the rectangle on the left are reflected to the inside of the rectangle on the right.

20. **A.** The black figures are reflected to the inside of the striped rectangle.

21. **E.** The patterns are identical in each row.

22. **B.** The puzzle piece completes the pattern.

23. **A.** The puzzle piece completes the pattern.

24. **E.** The puzzle piece completes the pattern.

25. D. The colors of the background and the figures exchange from left to right.

26. E. Across each row, the figures rotate 90 DEGREES clockwise. Down each column, the figures rotate 90 degrees counterclockwise.

27. A. The interior figures increase substantially in size from left to right.

28. D. The color/shade of the outer ring alternates across the row but stays the same down each column. Across the row, the number and position of diamonds change. Down the column, the diamonds change position.

29. A. The background color/shade and polygon alternate across and down.

30. B. The number of shapes in the boxes increase by one from left to right. Down each column, the number of shapes alternates.

31. A. Moving across the row from the left to center box, an inner (smaller) white shape is added (same shape as original). Moving from the center to right box, another inner (smaller) shape (of the original color) is added inside the white shape.

32. E. The shapes fold on the appropriate vertical and horizontal axes so that the outward points reflect inward, forming the new shape on the right.

33. D. The stacking order reverses on the right.

34. B. The puzzle piece completes the pattern.

35. E. The puzzle piece completes the pattern.

36. A. The puzzle piece completes the pattern.

37. B. The figures rotate counterclockwise from left to right.

38. C. The figures reflect on the horizontal axis from left to right.

39. D. The figures reflect on the vertical plane from left to right while the shapes and backgrounds alternate in color.

40. D. The shapes combine in each row from left to right to become the element in the third column. The second element turns from black to white in the combination shape.

41. B. The pentagon moves counterclockwise while the square stays in the same corner in each row. The square and pentagon overlap once in each row with the pentagon on top of the square.

42. D. The shapes in the top row are all pointing upwards, in the middle row downwards, and in the bottom row to the left.

43. E. The figures become larger and move from left to right across each row but do not expand beyond or touch the bounding box.

44. A. The lines rotate 180 degrees while the background color and color of the lines are inverted.

45. B. The figures are reflected along the horizontal axis while the background changes color.

46. E. The background shapes alternate between large, middle and small across and down.

47. B. Vertically and horizontally, the background shapes rotate 90 degrees clockwise while the foreground star rotates 45 degrees.

48. C. The shapes combine left to right across the rows and top to bottom of the columns.

DOWNLOAD THE PRACTICE TEST
IN COLOR

If you also want the COLOR version of this book, please go to the following link to download it!

Please visit
https://originstutoring.lpages.co/nnat130
to access a color version of your practice test.

Thank you for selecting this book. We would be thrilled if you left us a review on the website where you bought this book!

www.ingramcontent.com/pod-product-compliance
Lightning Source LLC
Chambersburg PA
CBHW080024130526
44591CB00036B/2640